2-Digi Addition(1)

```
     3          51           5           8
  + 80        + 27        + 12        + 15


     1           1           8           8
  + 84        + 67        +  3        +  4


    95           7          69          78
  +  1        +  6        +  2        +  6


    84          63          45           8
  +  4        +  6        + 29        +  3


    58          54          88           1
  + 45        +  1        + 48        +  6
```

2-Digi Addition(2)

72 + 88	69 + 92	37 + 37	76 + 60
48 + 41	26 + 45	19 + 43	70 + 85
13 + 47	79 + 60	61 + 10	22 + 79
67 + 54	24 + 43	25 + 50	18 + 83
12 + 62	22 + 84	88 + 15	94 + 54

2-Digi Addition(3)

```
   32          7         47          5
 + 37        + 9       + 18        + 5
```

```
   18          5          2          3
 +  7        + 4       + 59        + 4
```

```
    5          9         73         48
 +  8        +11       +  3        + 5
```

```
   52         66          9         67
 + 61        +41       +  1        +50
```

```
    9         99         52         34
 + 82        + 3       +  5        + 1
```

2-Digi Addition(4)

40 + 13	69 + 38	40 + 16	25 + 83
86 + 55	70 + 10	33 + 14	21 + 96
79 + 88	79 + 74	87 + 41	62 + 76
71 + 52	42 + 83	98 + 63	59 + 50
52 + 33	46 + 98	93 + 28	52 + 82

Name: _____

2-Digi Addition(5)

6 + 6	5 + 57	7 + 4	7 + 8
94 + 4	8 + 8	7 + 91	9 + 6
3 + 9	4 + 64	33 + 25	87 + 92
51 + 8	45 + 9	1 + 48	94 + 3
3 + 9	1 + 8	1 + 4	53 + 6

2-Digi Addition(6)

86 + 86	62 + 98	41 + 94	20 + 24
49 + 85	16 + 94	82 + 79	71 + 85
22 + 64	86 + 89	22 + 72	23 + 54
41 + 69	84 + 11	24 + 38	97 + 21
45 + 73	43 + 47	60 + 23	94 + 56

Name: _____

2-Digi Addition(7)

8 + 24	88 + 9	55 + 33	17 + 8
50 + 9	3 + 66	72 + 7	7 + 38
2 + 37	50 + 2	65 + 3	4 + 36
43 + 7	64 + 1	8 + 8	61 + 8
90 + 4	3 + 98	74 + 57	73 + 5

2-Digi Addition(8)

58 + 87	22 + 2	64 + 1	48 + 91
66 + 26	77 + 2	35 + 73	36 + 57
86 + 23	83 + 67	60 + 3	82 + 5
83 + 88	75 + 38	36 + 26	27 + 91
60 + 2	69 + 6	79 + 7	21 + 38

2-Digi Addition(9)

4 + 2	92 + 54	3 + 77	89 + 1
97 + 7	9 + 36	7 + 85	58 + 8
8 + 86	19 + 94	90 + 8	65 + 21
26 + 82	32 + 6	1 + 92	4 + 92
6 + 6	20 + 4	6 + 39	42 + 18

Name: _____

2-Digi Addition(10)

20 + 47	97 + 59	25 + 53	94 + 40
57 + 76	68 + 80	36 + 82	21 + 34
40 + 29	91 + 19	25 + 60	27 + 23
54 + 15	86 + 13	47 + 93	58 + 98
32 + 69	14 + 55	60 + 88	61 + 80

2-Digi Addition(1)

```
    3        51         5         8
+ 80      + 27      + 12      + 15
  83        78        17        23


    1         1         8         8
+ 84      + 67      +  3      +  4
  85        68        11        12


   95         7        69        78
+  1       +  6      +  2      +  6
  96        13        71        84


   84        63        45         8
+  4       +  6      + 29      +  3
  88        69        74        11


   58        54        88         1
+ 45       +  1      + 48      +  6
 103        55       136         7
```

A Ant

2-Digi Addition(2)

72 + 88 **160**	69 + 92 **161**	37 + 37 **74**	76 + 60 **136**
48 + 41 **89**	26 + 45 **71**	19 + 43 **62**	70 + 85 **155**
13 + 47 **60**	79 + 60 **139**	61 + 10 **71**	22 + 79 **101**
67 + 54 **121**	24 + 43 **67**	25 + 50 **75**	18 + 83 **101**
12 + 62 **74**	22 + 84 **106**	88 + 15 **103**	94 + 54 **148**

B Butterfly

2-Digi Addition(3)

```
   32          7         47          5
 + 37        + 9       + 18        + 5
   69         16         65         10


   18          5          2          3
 +  7        + 4       + 59        + 4
   25          9         61          7


    5          9         73         48
 +  8        +11       +  3        + 5
   13         20         76         53


   52         66          9         67
 + 61        +41       +  1        + 50
  113        107         10        117


    9         99         52         34
 + 82        + 3       +  5        + 1
   91        102         57         35
```

C
Cat

2-Digi Addition(4)

40 + 13 **53**	69 + 38 **107**	40 + 16 **56**	25 + 83 **108**
86 + 55 **141**	70 + 10 **80**	33 + 14 **47**	21 + 96 **117**
79 + 88 **167**	79 + 74 **153**	87 + 41 **128**	62 + 76 **138**
71 + 52 **123**	42 + 83 **125**	98 + 63 **161**	59 + 50 **109**
52 + 33 **85**	46 + 98 **144**	93 + 28 **121**	52 + 82 **134**

D
Dog

2-Digi Addition(5)

```
      6            5            7            7
  +   6        + 5 7        +   4        +   8
    1 2          6 2          1 1          1 5


    9 4            8            7            9
  +   4        +   8        + 9 1        +   6
    9 8          1 6          9 8          1 5


      3            4          3 3          8 7
  +   9        + 6 4        + 2 5        + 9 2
    1 2          6 8          5 8        1 7 9


    5 1          4 5            1          9 4
  +   8        +   9        + 4 8        +   3
    5 9          5 4          4 9          9 7


      3            1            1          5 3
  +   9        +   8        +   4        +   6
    1 2            9            5          5 9
```

E Elephant

2-Digi Addition(6)

```
   86        62        41        20
 + 86      + 98      + 94      + 24
 172       160       135        44
```

```
   49        16        82        71
 + 85      + 94      + 79      + 85
 134       110       161       156
```

```
   22        86        22        23
 + 64      + 89      + 72      + 54
  86       175        94        77
```

```
   41        84        24        97
 + 69      + 11      + 38      + 21
 110        95        62       118
```

```
   45        43        60        94
 + 73      + 47      + 23      + 56
 118        90        83       150
```

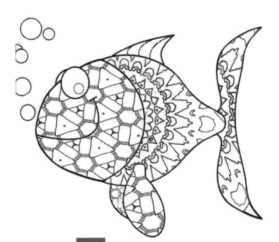

F Fish

2-Digi Addition(7)

```
    8          88          55          17
 + 24        +  9        + 33        +  8
   32          97          88          25


   50           3          72           7
 +  9        + 66        +  7        + 38
   59          69          79          45


    2          50          65           4
 + 37        +  2        +  3        + 36
   39          52          68          40


   43          64           8          61
 +  7        +  1        +  8        +  8
   50          65          16          69


   90           3          74          73
 +  4        + 98        + 57        +  5
   94         101         131          78
```

G
Giraffe

2-Digi Addition(8)

58 + 87 **145**	22 + 2 **24**	64 + 1 **65**	48 + 91 **139**
66 + 26 **92**	77 + 2 **79**	35 + 73 **108**	36 + 57 **93**
86 + 23 **109**	83 + 67 **150**	60 + 3 **63**	82 + 5 **87**
83 + 88 **171**	75 + 38 **113**	36 + 26 **62**	27 + 91 **118**
60 + 2 **62**	69 + 6 **75**	79 + 7 **86**	21 + 38 **59**

H Horse

2-Digi Addition(9)

```
    4          92           3          89
+   2        + 54        + 77         +  1
    6         146          80          90


   97           9           7          58
+   7        + 36        + 85        +  8
  104          45          92          66


    8          19          90          65
+  86        + 94        +  8        + 21
   94         113          98          86


   26          32           1           4
+  82        +  6        + 92        + 92
  108          38          93          96


    6          20           6          42
+   6        +  4        + 39        + 18
   12          24          45          60
```

 **Insect**

2-Digi Addition(10)

```
    20          97          25          94
  + 47        + 59        + 53        + 40
    67         156          78         134


    57          68          36          21
  + 76        + 80        + 82        + 34
   133         148         118          55


    40          91          25          27
  + 29        + 19        + 60        + 23
    69         110          85          50


    54          86          47          58
  + 15        + 13        + 93        + 98
    69          99         140         156


    32          14          60          61
  + 69        + 55        + 88        + 80
   101          69         148         141
```

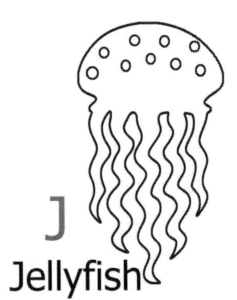

J
Jellyfish

Name: _____

2-Digi Subtraction(1)

78 − 19	28 − 15	21 − 10	44 − 26
60 − 25	40 − 16	15 − 6	92 − 40
91 − 41	20 − 17	54 − 4	10 − 3
97 − 64	70 − 44	68 − 22	59 − 56
84 − 67	22 − 11	68 − 17	32 − 16

2-Digi Subtraction(2)

$$\begin{array}{r} 92 \\ -\ 36 \\ \hline \end{array} \qquad \begin{array}{r} 38 \\ -\ 15 \\ \hline \end{array} \qquad \begin{array}{r} 28 \\ -\ 17 \\ \hline \end{array} \qquad \begin{array}{r} 24 \\ -\ 19 \\ \hline \end{array}$$

$$\begin{array}{r} 80 \\ -\ 25 \\ \hline \end{array} \qquad \begin{array}{r} 34 \\ -\ 26 \\ \hline \end{array} \qquad \begin{array}{r} 26 \\ -\ 24 \\ \hline \end{array} \qquad \begin{array}{r} 81 \\ -\ 75 \\ \hline \end{array}$$

$$\begin{array}{r} 78 \\ -\ 40 \\ \hline \end{array} \qquad \begin{array}{r} 68 \\ -\ 66 \\ \hline \end{array} \qquad \begin{array}{r} 53 \\ -\ 18 \\ \hline \end{array} \qquad \begin{array}{r} 12 \\ -\ 10 \\ \hline \end{array}$$

$$\begin{array}{r} 87 \\ -\ 17 \\ \hline \end{array} \qquad \begin{array}{r} 66 \\ -\ 20 \\ \hline \end{array} \qquad \begin{array}{r} 21 \\ -\ 19 \\ \hline \end{array} \qquad \begin{array}{r} 71 \\ -\ 60 \\ \hline \end{array}$$

$$\begin{array}{r} 83 \\ -\ 31 \\ \hline \end{array} \qquad \begin{array}{r} 31 \\ -\ 27 \\ \hline \end{array} \qquad \begin{array}{r} 25 \\ -\ 10 \\ \hline \end{array} \qquad \begin{array}{r} 25 \\ -\ 12 \\ \hline \end{array}$$

2-Digi Subtraction(3)

10 - 10	59 - 13	85 - 17	34 - 16
74 - 35	33 - 32	53 - 21	38 - 21
38 - 22	61 - 43	92 - 80	88 - 75
45 - 25	67 - 52	57 - 24	80 - 62
64 - 36	79 - 36	56 - 2	11 - 10

Name: _____

2-Digi Subtraction(4)

5 - 3	1 - 1	71 - 53	31 - 30
9 - 2	84 - 61	6 - 4	7 - 6
4 - 1	68 - 61	73 - 45	4 - 1
2 - 1	83 - 28	35 - 6	37 - 36
34 - 21	36 - 4	70 - 46	78 - 13

2-Digi Subtraction(5)

19	79	84	99
- 19	- 51	- 11	- 15

21	76	29	55
- 10	- 22	- 18	- 23

55	78	58	71
- 14	- 30	- 45	- 13

47	21	20	14
- 27	- 21	- 12	- 13

19	21	73	27
- 18	- 11	- 71	- 23

2-Digi Subtraction(6)

86 - 46	10 - 10	37 - 32	38 - 11
26 - 26	96 - 55	28 - 23	28 - 28
21 - 11	99 - 51	15 - 14	45 - 41
72 - 23	38 - 25	27 - 20	56 - 31
43 - 13	10 - 10	27 - 26	28 - 18

Name: _____

2-Digi Subtraction(7)

55 - 16	17 - 17	78 - 63	45 - 36
65 - 61	19 - 19	17 - 17	28 - 12
63 - 16	30 - 23	25 - 18	40 - 27
74 - 28	29 - 13	39 - 14	71 - 65
69 - 16	51 - 32	64 - 10	63 - 38

2-Digi Subtraction(8)

63 − 50	38 − 12	55 − 32	78 − 77
71 − 51	39 − 24	84 − 66	56 − 25
44 − 38	99 − 95	39 − 23	97 − 88
33 − 22	89 − 38	77 − 58	56 − 54
45 − 21	44 − 13	55 − 48	43 − 36

Name: _____

2-Digi Subtraction(9)

13 - 10	59 - 20	93 - 91	83 - 65
38 - 13	96 - 13	86 - 26	51 - 42
21 - 15	26 - 17	89 - 62	11 - 10
58 - 56	99 - 89	58 - 52	55 - 48
50 - 10	84 - 26	15 - 12	96 - 86

Name: _____

2-Digi Subtraction(10)

13 - 10	32 - 1	76 - 32	11 - 10
84 - 20	95 - 53	92 - 59	18 - 6
55 - 53	61 - 20	49 - 33	41 - 35
50 - 32	62 - 54	26 - 22	31 - 24
26 - 23	89 - 84	12 - 12	97 - 72

2-Digi Subtraction(1)

```
   78          28          21          44
 - 19        - 15        - 10        - 26
   59          13          11          18


   60          40          15          92
 - 25        - 16        -  6        - 40
   35          24           9          52


   91          20          54          10
 - 41        - 17        -  4        -  3
   50           3          50           7


   97          70          68          59
 - 64        - 44        - 22        - 56
   33          26          46           3


   84          22          68          32
 - 67        - 11        - 17        - 16
   17          11          51          16
```

K Koala

2-Digi Subtraction(2)

92 - 36 **5 6**	38 - 15 **2 3**	28 - 17 **1 1**	24 - 19 **5**
80 - 25 **5 5**	34 - 26 **8**	26 - 24 **2**	81 - 75 **6**
78 - 40 **3 8**	68 - 66 **2**	53 - 18 **3 5**	12 - 10 **2**
87 - 17 **7 0**	66 - 20 **4 6**	21 - 19 **2**	71 - 60 **1 1**
83 - 31 **5 2**	31 - 27 **4**	25 - 10 **1 5**	25 - 12 **1 3**

L Lion

2-Digi Subtraction(3)

10 - 10 **0**	59 - 13 **46**	85 - 17 **68**	34 - 16 **18**
74 - 35 **39**	33 - 32 **1**	53 - 21 **32**	38 - 21 **17**
38 - 22 **16**	61 - 43 **18**	92 - 80 **12**	88 - 75 **13**
45 - 25 **20**	67 - 52 **15**	57 - 24 **33**	80 - 62 **18**
64 - 36 **28**	79 - 36 **43**	56 - 2 **54**	11 - 10 **1**

M Monkey

2-Digi Subtraction(4)

5 − 3 **2**	1 − 1 **0**	71 − 53 **18**	31 − 30 **1**
9 − 2 **7**	84 − 61 **23**	6 − 4 **2**	7 − 6 **1**
4 − 1 **3**	68 − 61 **7**	73 − 45 **28**	4 − 1 **3**
2 − 1 **1**	83 − 28 **55**	35 − 6 **29**	37 − 36 **1**
34 − 21 **13**	36 − 4 **32**	70 − 46 **24**	78 − 13 **65**

N **Narwhal**

2-Digi Subtraction(5)

19 - 19 **0**	79 - 51 **28**	84 - 11 **73**	99 - 15 **84**
21 - 10 **11**	76 - 22 **54**	29 - 18 **11**	55 - 23 **32**
55 - 14 **41**	78 - 30 **48**	58 - 45 **13**	71 - 13 **58**
47 - 27 **20**	21 - 21 **0**	20 - 12 **8**	14 - 13 **1**
19 - 18 **1**	21 - 11 **10**	73 - 71 **2**	27 - 23 **4**

O Owl

2-Digi Subtraction(6)

86 - 46 **40**	10 - 10 **0**	37 - 32 **5**	38 - 11 **27**
26 - 26 **0**	96 - 55 **41**	28 - 23 **5**	28 - 28 **0**
21 - 11 **10**	99 - 51 **48**	15 - 14 **1**	45 - 41 **4**
72 - 23 **49**	38 - 25 **13**	27 - 20 **7**	56 - 31 **25**
43 - 13 **30**	10 - 10 **0**	27 - 26 **1**	28 - 18 **10**

P Panda

2-Digi Subtraction(7)

55 - 16 **39**	17 - 17 **0**	78 - 63 **15**	45 - 36 **9**
65 - 61 **4**	19 - 19 **0**	17 - 17 **0**	28 - 12 **16**
63 - 16 **47**	30 - 23 **7**	25 - 18 **7**	40 - 27 **13**
74 - 28 **46**	29 - 13 **16**	39 - 14 **25**	71 - 65 **6**
69 - 16 **53**	51 - 32 **19**	64 - 10 **54**	63 - 38 **25**

Q Queen Bee

2-Digi Subtraction(8)

63 - 50 **13**	38 - 12 **26**	55 - 32 **23**	78 - 77 **1**
71 - 51 **20**	39 - 24 **15**	84 - 66 **18**	56 - 25 **31**
44 - 38 **6**	99 - 95 **4**	39 - 23 **16**	97 - 88 **9**
33 - 22 **11**	89 - 38 **51**	77 - 58 **19**	56 - 54 **2**
45 - 21 **24**	44 - 13 **31**	55 - 48 **7**	43 - 36 **7**

R Rabbit

2-Digi Subtraction(9)

13 − 10 **3**	59 − 20 **39**	93 − 91 **2**	83 − 65 **18**
38 − 13 **25**	96 − 13 **83**	86 − 26 **60**	51 − 42 **9**
21 − 15 **6**	26 − 17 **9**	89 − 62 **27**	11 − 10 **1**
58 − 56 **2**	99 − 89 **10**	58 − 52 **6**	55 − 48 **7**
50 − 10 **40**	84 − 26 **58**	15 − 12 **3**	96 − 86 **10**

S Sheep

2-Digi Subtraction(10)

```
  13        32        76        11
- 10      -  1      - 32      - 10
   3        31        44         1


  84        95        92        18
- 20      - 53      - 59      -  6
  64        42        33        12


  55        61        49        41
- 53      - 20      - 33      - 35
   2        41        16         6


  50        62        26        31
- 32      - 54      - 22      - 24
  18         8         4         7


  26        89        12        97
- 23      - 84      - 12      - 72
   3         5         0        25
```

T Tiger

Name: _____

3-Digi Addition(1)

```
  611        127        226        662
+   6      +   4      +  60      + 513
```

```
  946        986        720        795
+   9      +  47      + 853      +   2
```

```
  458        426        849        333
+   1      +   2      +   5      +  59
```

```
  118        912        827        298
+   6      +  95      +  18      +  32
```

```
  493        612        763        147
+   4      +   4      +   7      + 942
```

3-Digi Addition(2)

```
  473        619        445        856
+  46      +  77      + 528      +  77
```

```
  455        504        419        362
+ 830      + 651      +  27      +  57
```

```
  249        364        744        679
+ 436      + 971      +  52      + 662
```

```
  868        795        156        268
+  89      + 439      +  64      + 981
```

```
  612        547        793        491
+  40      + 204      + 533      + 844
```

Name: _____

3-Digi Addition(3)

982 + 93	533 + 62	305 + 72	850 + 413
277 + 56	733 + 81	496 + 81	792 + 10
940 + 945	902 + 73	324 + 82	240 + 94
638 + 50	773 + 95	368 + 54	345 + 312
379 + 99	381 + 50	608 + 897	810 + 94

Name: _____

3-Digi Addition(4)

947 + 291	180 + 839	166 + 41	158 + 644
729 + 49	437 + 57	843 + 56	239 + 563
340 + 817	384 + 46	196 + 928	602 + 75
762 + 481	523 + 931	533 + 590	734 + 62
894 + 869	582 + 31	134 + 255	151 + 759

Name: _____

3-Digi Addition(5)

718 + 429	829 + 275	406 + 591	295 + 69
856 + 361	511 + 755	981 + 432	363 + 73
818 + 21	531 + 47	411 + 77	818 + 141
555 + 48	183 + 266	333 + 22	556 + 831
526 + 44	876 + 223	914 + 348	772 + 528

3-Digi Addition(6)

550 + 562	616 + 173	698 + 508	364 + 215
126 + 908	572 + 155	391 + 747	545 + 975
650 + 738	578 + 199	236 + 760	398 + 640
773 + 139	672 + 548	916 + 690	927 + 181
209 + 378	125 + 920	869 + 785	387 + 177

3-Digi Addition(7)

787 + 323	322 + 197	947 + 246	624 + 980
613 + 981	320 + 520	519 + 527	928 + 624
578 + 413	808 + 157	938 + 814	234 + 333
495 + 925	164 + 450	532 + 423	700 + 623
604 + 321	998 + 931	197 + 984	921 + 142

Name: _____

3-Digi Addition(8)

```
    17          787          60           33
  +  99        +  50       + 696       + 228
```

```
   982          767          89           72
  +  57        +  56       +  50       + 806
```

```
   551          326          96           77
  +  76        +  35       + 439       +  43
```

```
    68          709          93          769
  + 139        + 999       + 713       + 663
```

```
    42          711          76           50
  +  20        + 513       +  92       + 532
```

3-Digi Addition(9)

740 + 405	658 + 216	495 + 395	613 + 645
857 + 477	744 + 583	198 + 894	844 + 192
789 + 954	425 + 379	125 + 668	134 + 637
744 + 821	189 + 500	656 + 768	231 + 286
968 + 732	643 + 765	482 + 746	880 + 914

3-Digi Addition(10)

637 + 680	680 + 674	371 + 535	585 + 336
552 + 422	730 + 353	661 + 387	503 + 779
209 + 919	352 + 760	762 + 178	717 + 772
683 + 568	213 + 207	163 + 420	375 + 837
113 + 712	919 + 981	470 + 219	184 + 554

3-Digi Addition(1)

```
   611          127          226          662
 +   6        +   4        +  60        + 513
   617          131          286        1,175
```

```
   946          986          720          795
 +   9        +  47        + 853        +   2
   955        1,033        1,573          797
```

```
   458          426          849          333
 +   1        +   2        +   5        +  59
   459          428          854          392
```

```
   118          912          827          298
 +   6        +  95        +  18        +  32
   124        1,007          845          330
```

```
   493          612          763          147
 +   4        +   4        +   7        + 942
   497          616          770        1,089
```

U
Unicorn

3-Digi Addition(2)

```
   473          619          445          856
 +  46        +  77        + 528        +  77
   519          696          973          933


   455          504          419          362
 + 830        + 651        +  27        +  57
 1,285        1,155          446          419


   249          364          744          679
 + 436        + 971        +  52        + 662
   685        1,335          796        1,341


   868          795          156          268
 +  89        + 439        +  64        + 981
   957        1,234          220        1,249


   612          547          793          491
 +  40        + 204        + 533        + 844
   652          751        1,326        1,335
```

V vulture

3-Digi Addition(3)

```
   982          533          305          850
 +  93        +  62        +  72        + 413
 1,075          595          377        1,263
```

```
   277          733          496          792
 +  56        +  81        +  81        +  10
   333          814          577          802
```

```
   940          902          324          240
 + 945        +  73        +  82        +  94
 1,885          975          406          334
```

```
   638          773          368          345
 +  50        +  95        +  54        + 312
   688          868          422          657
```

```
   379          381          608          810
 +  99        +  50        + 897        +  94
   478          431        1,505          904
```

W

Walrus

3-Digi Addition(4)

947 + 291 **1,238**	180 + 839 **1,019**	166 + 41 **207**	158 + 644 **802**
729 + 49 **778**	437 + 57 **494**	843 + 56 **899**	239 + 563 **802**
340 + 817 **1,157**	384 + 46 **430**	196 + 928 **1,124**	602 + 75 **677**
762 + 481 **1,243**	523 + 931 **1,454**	533 + 590 **1,123**	734 + 62 **796**
894 + 869 **1,763**	582 + 31 **613**	134 + 255 **389**	151 + 759 **910**

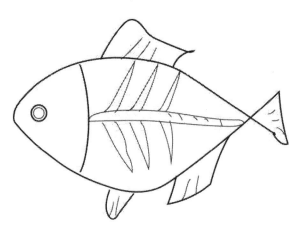

 x ray fish

3-Digi Addition(5)

```
  718        829        406        295
+ 429      + 275      + 591      +  69
─────      ─────      ─────      ─────
1,147      1,104        997        364


  856        511        981        363
+ 361      + 755      + 432      +  73
─────      ─────      ─────      ─────
1,217      1,266      1,413        436


  818        531        411        818
+  21      +  47      +  77      + 141
─────      ─────      ─────      ─────
  839        578        488        959


  555        183        333        556
+  48      + 266      +  22      + 831
─────      ─────      ─────      ─────
  603        449        355      1,387


  526        876        914        772
+  44      + 223      + 348      + 528
─────      ─────      ─────      ─────
  570      1,099      1,262      1,300
```

Y Yak

3-Digi Addition(6)

550 + 562 **1,112**	616 + 173 **789**	698 + 508 **1,206**	364 + 215 **579**
126 + 908 **1,034**	572 + 155 **727**	391 + 747 **1,138**	545 + 975 **1,520**
650 + 738 **1,388**	578 + 199 **777**	236 + 760 **996**	398 + 640 **1,038**
773 + 139 **912**	672 + 548 **1,220**	916 + 690 **1,606**	927 + 181 **1,108**
209 + 378 **587**	125 + 920 **1,045**	869 + 785 **1,654**	387 + 177 **564**

Z Zebra

3-Digi Addition(7)

```
   787          322          947          624
 + 323        + 197        + 246        + 980
 1,110          519        1,193        1,604


   613          320          519          928
 + 981        + 520        + 527        + 624
 1,594          840        1,046        1,552


   578          808          938          234
 + 413        + 157        + 814        + 333
   991          965        1,752          567


   495          164          532          700
 + 925        + 450        + 423        + 623
 1,420          614          955        1,323


   604          998          197          921
 + 321        + 931        + 984        + 142
   925        1,929        1,181        1,063
```

One

3-Digi Addition(8)

```
    17          787          60           33
+   99       +   50      +  696       +  228
  116          837         756          261


   982          767          89           72
+   57       +   56      +   50       +  806
 1,039          823         139          878


   551          326          96           77
+   76       +   35      +  439       +   43
   627          361         535          120


    68          709          93          769
+  139       +  999      +  713       +  663
   207        1,708         806        1,432


    42          711          76           50
+   20       +  513      +   92       +  532
    62        1,224         168          582
```

2

Two

3-Digi Addition(9)

```
   740          658          495          613
 + 405        + 216        + 395        + 645
 1,145          874          890        1,258


   857          744          198          844
 + 477        + 583        + 894        + 192
 1,334        1,327        1,092        1,036


   789          425          125          134
 + 954        + 379        + 668        + 637
 1,743          804          793          771


   744          189          656          231
 + 821        + 500        + 768        + 286
 1,565          689        1,424          517


   968          643          482          880
 + 732        + 765        + 746        + 914
 1,700        1,408        1,228        1,794
```

Three

3-Digi Addition(10)

```
  637          680          371          585
+ 680        + 674        + 535        + 336
1,317        1,354          906          921


  552          730          661          503
+ 422        + 353        + 387        + 779
  974        1,083        1,048        1,282


  209          352          762          717
+ 919        + 760        + 178        + 772
1,128        1,112          940        1,489


  683          213          163          375
+ 568        + 207        + 420        + 837
1,251          420          583        1,212


  113          919          470          184
+ 712        + 981        + 219        + 554
  825        1,900          689          738
```

Four

Name: _____

3-Digi Subtraction(1)

390 - 352	845 - 229	648 - 262	611 - 341
272 - 209	260 - 212	629 - 501	751 - 493
963 - 579	583 - 370	733 - 386	711 - 16
326 - 112	761 - 455	257 - 172	451 - 221
482 - 414	175 - 151	340 - 264	171 - 110

3-Digi Subtraction(2)

486 - 291	530 - 501	413 - 279	611 - 69
422 - 135	780 - 521	332 - 276	853 - 502
383 - 317	653 - 506	586 - 131	825 - 363
598 - 315	587 - 169	819 - 205	883 - 477
996 - 600	729 - 497	947 - 940	538 - 391

Name: _____

3-Digi Subtraction(3)

387	954	119	976
- 336	- 777	- 102	- 402

162	996	392	860
- 146	- 911	- 325	- 303

780	290	838	419
- 357	- 220	- 532	- 291

862	738	779	123
- 211	- 531	- 430	- 110

420	331	443	328
- 320	- 268	- 114	- 224

Name: _____

3-Digi Subtraction(4)

125 - 121	725 - 228	927 - 261	966 - 466
594 - 571	448 - 323	131 - 128	863 - 421
903 - 530	351 - 157	198 - 178	989 - 542
573 - 313	553 - 417	943 - 932	835 - 599
819 - 669	135 - 103	159 - 152	560 - 409

3-Digi Subtraction(5)

435 - 229	334 - 251	873 - 290	865 - 479
444 - 176	199 - 110	817 - 800	148 - 128
611 - 287	117 - 108	780 - 123	588 - 354
217 - 102	747 - 739	777 - 606	734 - 506
718 - 669	866 - 753	973 - 295	577 - 326

Name: _____

3-Digi Subtraction(6)

485	509	128	811
- 123	- 109	- 128	- 729

642	253	795	776
- 414	- 150	- 54	- 412

514	247	144	407
- 211	- 205	- 132	- 83

650	190	470	851
- 354	- 110	- 177	- 509

114	560	955	620
- 101	- 126	- 710	- 359

Name: _____

3-Digi Subtraction(7)

213	450	893	473
- 85	- 105	- 115	- 378

544	365	738	452
- 427	- 103	- 480	- 266

418	516	200	301
- 311	- 317	- 33	- 184

480	997	368	420
- 235	- 761	- 209	- 41

341	954	674	969
- 267	- 83	- 314	- 125

Name: _____

3-Digi Subtraction(8)

375 - 41	286 - 225	164 - 121	454 - 15
813 - 723	171 - 162	986 - 554	710 - 18
980 - 162	378 - 355	131 - 41	881 - 100
758 - 656	636 - 475	812 - 688	512 - 499
224 - 154	269 - 175	415 - 209	428 - 169

3-Digi Subtraction(9)

382 - 166	900 - 576	135 - 110	696 - 117
142 - 133	826 - 782	373 - 187	255 - 202
700 - 128	758 - 277	839 - 625	900 - 327
341 - 326	681 - 352	606 - 523	184 - 163
808 - 289	219 - 114	632 - 117	590 - 586

3-Digi Subtraction(10)

121	209	929	292
- 58	- 93	- 344	- 234

711	114	945	919
- 452	- 112	- 407	- 902

623	510	232	614
- 567	- 328	- 122	- 364

409	507	955	935
- 118	- 117	- 885	- 415

556	314	235	957
- 280	- 238	- 225	- 575

3-Digi Subtraction(1)

```
  390          845          648          611
- 352        - 229        - 262        - 341
   38          616          386          270


  272          260          629          751
- 209        - 212        - 501        - 493
   63           48          128          258


  963          583          733          711
- 579        - 370        - 386        -  16
  384          213          347          695


  326          761          257          451
- 112        - 455        - 172        - 221
  214          306           85          230


  482          175          340          171
- 414        - 151        - 264        - 110
   68           24           76           61
```

Five

3-Digi Subtraction(2)

```
  486          530          413          611
- 291        - 501        - 279        -  69
  195           29          134          542
```

```
  422          780          332          853
- 135        - 521        - 276        - 502
  287          259           56          351
```

```
  383          653          586          825
- 317        - 506        - 131        - 363
   66          147          455          462
```

```
  598          587          819          883
- 315        - 169        - 205        - 477
  283          418          614          406
```

```
  996          729          947          538
- 600        - 497        - 940        - 391
  396          232            7          147
```

Six

3-Digi Subtraction(3)

```
  387        954        119        976
- 336      - 777      - 102      - 402
   51        177         17        574


  162        996        392        860
- 146      - 911      - 325      - 303
   16         85         67        557


  780        290        838        419
- 357      - 220      - 532      - 291
  423         70        306        128


  862        738        779        123
- 211      - 531      - 430      - 110
  651        207        349         13


  420        331        443        328
- 320      - 268      - 114      - 224
  100         63        329        104
```

Seven

3-Digi Subtraction(4)

```
  125        725        927        966
- 121      - 228      - 261      - 466
    4        497        666        500


  594        448        131        863
- 571      - 323      - 128      - 421
   23        125          3        442


  903        351        198        989
- 530      - 157      - 178      - 542
  373        194         20        447


  573        553        943        835
- 313      - 417      - 932      - 599
  260        136         11        236


  819        135        159        560
- 669      - 103      - 152      - 409
  150         32          7        151
```

8

Eight

3-Digi Subtraction(5)

```
   435        334        873        865
 - 229      - 251      - 290      - 479
   206         83        583        386


   444        199        817        148
 - 176      - 110      - 800      - 128
   268         89         17         20


   611        117        780        588
 - 287      - 108      - 123      - 354
   324          9        657        234


   217        747        777        734
 - 102      - 739      - 606      - 506
   115          8        171        228


   718        866        973        577
 - 669      - 753      - 295      - 326
    49        113        678        251
```

9

Nine

3-Digi Subtraction(6)

485 - 123 **362**	509 - 109 **400**	128 - 128 **0**	811 - 729 **82**
642 - 414 **228**	253 - 150 **103**	795 - 54 **741**	776 - 412 **364**
514 - 211 **303**	247 - 205 **42**	144 - 132 **12**	407 - 83 **324**
650 - 354 **296**	190 - 110 **80**	470 - 177 **293**	851 - 509 **342**
114 - 101 **13**	560 - 126 **434**	955 - 710 **245**	620 - 359 **261**

10
Ten

3-Digi Subtraction(7)

213 - 85 **128**	450 - 105 **345**	893 - 115 **778**	473 - 378 **95**
544 - 427 **117**	365 - 103 **262**	738 - 480 **258**	452 - 266 **186**
418 - 311 **107**	516 - 317 **199**	200 - 33 **167**	301 - 184 **117**
480 - 235 **245**	997 - 761 **236**	368 - 209 **159**	420 - 41 **379**
341 - 267 **74**	954 - 83 **871**	674 - 314 **360**	969 - 125 **844**

11

Eleven

3-Digi Subtraction(8)

375 − 41 **334**	286 − 225 **61**	164 − 121 **43**	454 − 15 **439**
813 − 723 **90**	171 − 162 **9**	986 − 554 **432**	710 − 18 **692**
980 − 162 **818**	378 − 355 **23**	131 − 41 **90**	881 − 100 **781**
758 − 656 **102**	636 − 475 **161**	812 − 688 **124**	512 − 499 **13**
224 − 154 **70**	269 − 175 **94**	415 − 209 **206**	428 − 169 **259**

Twelve

3-Digi Subtraction(9)

382 - 166 **216**	900 - 576 **324**	135 - 110 **25**	696 - 117 **579**
142 - 133 **9**	826 - 782 **44**	373 - 187 **186**	255 - 202 **53**
700 - 128 **572**	758 - 277 **481**	839 - 625 **214**	900 - 327 **573**
341 - 326 **15**	681 - 352 **329**	606 - 523 **83**	184 - 163 **21**
808 - 289 **519**	219 - 114 **105**	632 - 117 **515**	590 - 586 **4**

Thirteen

3-Digi Subtraction(10)

121 - 58 **63**	209 - 93 **116**	929 - 344 **585**	292 - 234 **58**
711 - 452 **259**	114 - 112 **2**	945 - 407 **538**	919 - 902 **17**
623 - 567 **56**	510 - 328 **182**	232 - 122 **110**	614 - 364 **250**
409 - 118 **291**	507 - 117 **390**	955 - 885 **70**	935 - 415 **520**
556 - 280 **276**	314 - 238 **76**	235 - 225 **10**	957 - 575 **382**

Fourteen

4-Digi Addition(1)

1,054 + 137	6,981 + 6,469	3,402 + 2,422	9,363 + 3,125

3,763 + 7,870	2,488 + 693	8,653 + 1,772	9,774 + 956

6,894 + 397	5,715 + 828	6,077 + 7,001	5,952 + 2,547

3,799 + 429	6,278 + 6,019	1,883 + 7,839	5,161 + 3,729

1,264 + 3,160	7,040 + 1,449	3,445 + 4,918	4,276 + 5,692

4-Digi Addition(2)

4,551	8,381	7,889	9,502
+ 480	+ 52	+ 52	+ 38

2,164	3,031	6,446	3,643
+ 27	+ 479	+ 1,925	+ 76

1,168	8,184	2,344	4,115
+ 698	+ 249	+ 6,421	+ 625

2,924	3,874	2,709	5,563
+ 2,469	+ 77	+ 70	+ 884

9,366	2,392	2,260	2,322
+ 2,506	+ 687	+ 9,765	+ 289

4-Digi Addition(3)

```
  1,126        4,849        8,687        2,637
+ 8,520      +   674      + 6,028      +   894
```

```
  4,531        4,531        8,043        1,098
+ 8,565      +   792      +   969      + 6,458
```

```
  8,085        3,160        1,487        7,439
+ 6,008      +   864      +   581      +   307
```

```
  6,515        5,561        6,949        8,041
+ 5,919      + 8,369      + 2,476      + 1,175
```

```
  6,444        7,471        1,569        6,580
+   837      + 1,491      + 9,005      + 1,397
```

4-Digi Addition(4)

3,150 + 2,400	1,706 + 8,371	4,664 + 6,629	5,081 + 4,370
1,431 + 2,818	5,913 + 8,054	6,404 + 9,164	5,685 + 9,593
6,933 + 1,941	4,584 + 6,680	6,856 + 9,632	7,419 + 1,526
6,459 + 6,936	9,500 + 7,993	9,207 + 7,387	8,462 + 2,734
1,847 + 5,423	4,731 + 1,153	7,233 + 2,857	7,684 + 4,907

4-Digi Addition(5)

3,754 + 5,470	8,999 + 2,628	3,209 + 5,142	5,178 + 6,422
6,678 + 1,875	7,132 + 6,906	7,819 + 5,312	7,924 + 1,545
7,025 + 5,123	1,746 + 6,785	9,424 + 9,388	9,401 + 8,028
1,519 + 5,729	3,489 + 9,491	2,457 + 4,431	7,122 + 6,918
1,687 + 9,109	4,408 + 3,166	6,505 + 2,850	4,542 + 5,376

4-Digi Addition(6)

1,900 + 2,100	3,279 + 2,063	5,885 + 9,974	4,404 + 8,135
6,226 + 5,316	8,286 + 3,367	6,668 + 8,596	8,400 + 6,947
9,445 + 9,175	2,136 + 3,405	4,346 + 1,326	5,095 + 4,731
4,772 + 6,571	2,779 + 3,809	7,527 + 2,826	1,342 + 6,004
8,274 + 8,766	3,900 + 6,244	8,778 + 2,690	5,362 + 7,344

4-Digi Addition(7)

4,609 + 4,650	1,663 + 7,167	5,818 + 984	6,055 + 785
6,227 + 188	8,458 + 4,121	2,342 + 503	2,856 + 290
7,179 + 6,410	7,711 + 9,559	8,632 + 420	1,966 + 7,665
4,889 + 294	7,800 + 172	3,688 + 525	2,014 + 4,656
5,208 + 218	3,451 + 574	9,980 + 206	8,697 + 1,184

Name: _____

4-Digi Addition(8)

2,563 + 3,927	6,650 + 6,225	2,454 + 371	6,772 + 428
9,822 + 9,848	3,867 + 903	5,368 + 728	3,809 + 397
4,069 + 2,803	5,667 + 323	1,603 + 657	4,563 + 2,696
7,247 + 957	6,977 + 5,281	1,212 + 2,523	1,226 + 8,765
8,401 + 885	9,487 + 1,759	1,154 + 5,842	4,685 + 192

4-Digi Addition(9)

6,873	4,657	4,385	2,528
+ 53	+ 4,403	+ 264	+ 281

9,065	6,270	7,179	5,926
+ 5,486	+ 528	+ 221	+ 7,663

2,614	5,297	5,174	2,402
+ 4,285	+ 2,758	+ 44	+ 135

1,487	1,942	3,364	9,399
+ 3,341	+ 642	+ 2,188	+ 2,964

2,705	8,330	6,848	1,347
+ 13	+ 96	+ 8,591	+ 684

4-Digi Addition(10)

7,609 + 53	4,970 + 64	8,240 + 12	7,761 + 8,931
5,421 + 91	6,482 + 558	4,030 + 68	2,308 + 115
8,226 + 243	6,593 + 767	3,400 + 302	2,600 + 64
2,694 + 161	9,936 + 933	2,822 + 7,584	5,701 + 8,540
6,076 + 48	9,818 + 5,436	1,969 + 99	7,932 + 236

4-Digi Addition(1)

```
  1,054          6,981          3,402          9,363
+   137        + 6,469        + 2,422        + 3,125
  1,191         13,450          5,824         12,488


  3,763          2,488          8,653          9,774
+ 7,870        +   693        + 1,772        +   956
 11,633          3,181         10,425         10,730


  6,894          5,715          6,077          5,952
+   397        +   828        + 7,001        + 2,547
  7,291          6,543         13,078          8,499


  3,799          6,278          1,883          5,161
+   429        + 6,019        + 7,839        + 3,729
  4,228         12,297          9,722          8,890


  1,264          7,040          3,445          4,276
+ 3,160        + 1,449        + 4,918        + 5,692
  4,424          8,489          8,363          9,968
```

Fifteen

4-Digi Addition(2)

```
   4,551          8,381          7,889          9,502
+    480        +    52        +    52        +    38
   5,031          8,433          7,941          9,540


   2,164          3,031          6,446          3,643
+     27        +   479        + 1,925        +    76
   2,191          3,510          8,371          3,719


   1,168          8,184          2,344          4,115
+    698        +   249        + 6,421        +   625
   1,866          8,433          8,765          4,740


   2,924          3,874          2,709          5,563
+  2,469        +    77        +    70        +   884
   5,393          3,951          2,779          6,447


   9,366          2,392          2,260          2,322
+  2,506        +   687        + 9,765        +   289
  11,872          3,079         12,025          2,611
```

16

Sixteen

4-Digi Addition(3)

```
  1,126        4,849        8,687        2,637
+ 8,520      +   674      + 6,028      +   894
  9,646        5,523       14,715        3,531


  4,531        4,531        8,043        1,098
+ 8,565      +   792      +   969      + 6,458
 13,096        5,323        9,012        7,556


  8,085        3,160        1,487        7,439
+ 6,008      +   864      +   581      +   307
 14,093        4,024        2,068        7,746


  6,515        5,561        6,949        8,041
+ 5,919      + 8,369      + 2,476      + 1,175
 12,434       13,930        9,425        9,216


  6,444        7,471        1,569        6,580
+   837      + 1,491      + 9,005      + 1,397
  7,281        8,962       10,574        7,977
```

Seventeen

4-Digi Addition(4)

```
  3,150        1,706        4,664        5,081
+ 2,400      + 8,371      + 6,629      + 4,370
  5,550       10,077       11,293        9,451


  1,431        5,913        6,404        5,685
+ 2,818      + 8,054      + 9,164      + 9,593
  4,249       13,967       15,568       15,278


  6,933        4,584        6,856        7,419
+ 1,941      + 6,680      + 9,632      + 1,526
  8,874       11,264       16,488        8,945


  6,459        9,500        9,207        8,462
+ 6,936      + 7,993      + 7,387      + 2,734
 13,395       17,493       16,594       11,196


  1,847        4,731        7,233        7,684
+ 5,423      + 1,153      + 2,857      + 4,907
  7,270        5,884       10,090       12,591
```

Eighteen

4-Digi Addition(5)

```
  3,754        8,999        3,209        5,178
+ 5,470      + 2,628      + 5,142      + 6,422
  9,224       11,627        8,351       11,600


  6,678        7,132        7,819        7,924
+ 1,875      + 6,906      + 5,312      + 1,545
  8,553       14,038       13,131        9,469


  7,025        1,746        9,424        9,401
+ 5,123      + 6,785      + 9,388      + 8,028
 12,148        8,531       18,812       17,429


  1,519        3,489        2,457        7,122
+ 5,729      + 9,491      + 4,431      + 6,918
  7,248       12,980        6,888       14,040


  1,687        4,408        6,505        4,542
+ 9,109      + 3,166      + 2,850      + 5,376
 10,796        7,574        9,355        9,918
```

19

Nineteen

4-Digi Addition(6)

1,900 + 2,100 **4,000**	3,279 + 2,063 **5,342**	5,885 + 9,974 **15,859**	4,404 + 8,135 **12,539**
6,226 + 5,316 **11,542**	8,286 + 3,367 **11,653**	6,668 + 8,596 **15,264**	8,400 + 6,947 **15,347**
9,445 + 9,175 **18,620**	2,136 + 3,405 **5,541**	4,346 + 1,326 **5,672**	5,095 + 4,731 **9,826**
4,772 + 6,571 **11,343**	2,779 + 3,809 **6,588**	7,527 + 2,826 **10,353**	1,342 + 6,004 **7,346**
8,274 + 8,766 **17,040**	3,900 + 6,244 **10,144**	8,778 + 2,690 **11,468**	5,362 + 7,344 **12,706**

Twenty

4-Digi Addition(7)

4,609 + 4,650 **9,259**	1,663 + 7,167 **8,830**	5,818 + 984 **6,802**	6,055 + 785 **6,840**
6,227 + 188 **6,415**	8,458 + 4,121 **12,579**	2,342 + 503 **2,845**	2,856 + 290 **3,146**
7,179 + 6,410 **13,589**	7,711 + 9,559 **17,270**	8,632 + 420 **9,052**	1,966 + 7,665 **9,631**
4,889 + 294 **5,183**	7,800 + 172 **7,972**	3,688 + 525 **4,213**	2,014 + 4,656 **6,670**
5,208 + 218 **5,426**	3,451 + 574 **4,025**	9,980 + 206 **10,186**	8,697 + 1,184 **9,881**

21

Twenty- One

4-Digi Addition(8)

2,563 + 3,927 **6,490**	6,650 + 6,225 **12,875**	2,454 + 371 **2,825**	6,772 + 428 **7,200**
9,822 + 9,848 **19,670**	3,867 + 903 **4,770**	5,368 + 728 **6,096**	3,809 + 397 **4,206**
4,069 + 2,803 **6,872**	5,667 + 323 **5,990**	1,603 + 657 **2,260**	4,563 + 2,696 **7,259**
7,247 + 957 **8,204**	6,977 + 5,281 **12,258**	1,212 + 2,523 **3,735**	1,226 + 8,765 **9,991**
8,401 + 885 **9,286**	9,487 + 1,759 **11,246**	1,154 + 5,842 **6,996**	4,685 + 192 **4,877**

22

Twenty-Two

4-Digi Addition(9)

```
  6,873          4,657          4,385          2,528
+    53        + 4,403        +   264        +   281
 6,926          9,060          4,649          2,809


  9,065          6,270          7,179          5,926
+ 5,486        +   528        +   221        + 7,663
 14,551         6,798          7,400         13,589


  2,614          5,297          5,174          2,402
+ 4,285        + 2,758        +    44        +   135
 6,899          8,055          5,218          2,537


  1,487          1,942          3,364          9,399
+ 3,341        +   642        + 2,188        + 2,964
 4,828          2,584          5,552         12,363


  2,705          8,330          6,848          1,347
+    13        +    96        + 8,591        +   684
 2,718          8,426         15,439          2,031
```

Twenty-Three

4-Digi Addition(10)

7,609 + 53 **7,662**	4,970 + 64 **5,034**	8,240 + 12 **8,252**	7,761 + 8,931 **16,692**
5,421 + 91 **5,512**	6,482 + 558 **7,040**	4,030 + 68 **4,098**	2,308 + 115 **2,423**
8,226 + 243 **8,469**	6,593 + 767 **7,360**	3,400 + 302 **3,702**	2,600 + 64 **2,664**
2,694 + 161 **2,855**	9,936 + 933 **10,869**	2,822 + 7,584 **10,406**	5,701 + 8,540 **14,241**
6,076 + 48 **6,124**	9,818 + 5,436 **15,254**	1,969 + 99 **2,068**	7,932 + 236 **8,168**

24

Twenty-Four

4-Digi Subtraction(1)

5,925 - 2,317	2,694 - 2,424	3,648 - 3,543	7,439 - 435
5,398 - 1,360	5,605 - 2,207	3,101 - 762	7,771 - 2,206
6,642 - 167	2,868 - 1,909	3,849 - 3,383	1,051 - 1,030
2,954 - 1,584	2,128 - 1,043	3,570 - 361	7,298 - 3,828
6,993 - 4,865	8,825 - 7,006	7,187 - 5,469	4,330 - 2,880

4-Digi Subtraction(2)

3,250	9,843	4,134	4,508
− 209	− 1,626	− 2,479	− 1,580

1,286	2,767	7,841	9,519
− 1,199	− 1,480	− 2,299	− 5,273

6,227	1,784	5,245	7,948
− 3,591	− 611	− 2,576	− 3,414

3,560	4,818	2,464	9,870
− 531	− 2,215	− 1,984	− 1,178

9,005	9,380	7,748	8,401
− 1,356	− 8,459	− 7,120	− 2,280

4-Digi Subtraction(3)

```
  9,717      8,622      9,163      3,228
- 7,350    - 1,897    - 2,838    - 1,751
```

```
  3,306      2,594      6,671      5,714
- 3,286    - 1,038    - 4,567    - 5,123
```

```
  4,978      4,062      4,676      8,170
- 2,407    -   852    - 2,573    - 4,483
```

```
  1,200      5,881      3,672      4,342
- 1,028    - 5,548    - 2,612    - 3,640
```

```
  7,617      7,942      1,982      4,006
- 6,038    - 6,530    -   622    - 1,177
```

Name: _____

4-Digi Subtraction(4)

8,997 - 4,666	8,964 - 4,495	9,298 - 7,418	7,150 - 6,432
5,420 - 4,459	4,912 - 3,974	9,907 - 3,640	2,094 - 1,204
9,447 - 5,487	6,606 - 6,410	2,850 - 1,762	3,824 - 2,981
7,428 - 5,669	6,403 - 2,186	3,551 - 601	7,831 - 2,694
8,906 - 8,041	4,457 - 1,411	6,853 - 6,761	9,738 - 1,934

4-Digi Subtraction(5)

2,654 - 2,116	547 - 494	618 - 541	320 - 188
3,797 - 2,390	500 - 278	727 - 698	301 - 136
8,529 - 3,316	2,153 - 2,083	375 - 139	182 - 34
9,329 - 398	662 - 40	6,103 - 4,154	1,001 - 184
2,062 - 1,432	1,323 - 1,122	7,218 - 4,832	450 - 23

Name: _____

4-Digi Subtraction(6)

3,514	7,511	3,453	9,973
− 1,207	− 3,116	− 1,047	− 1,410

2,594	4,664	6,102	7,681
− 2,334	− 2,274	− 5,818	− 3,963

4,626	7,914	5,436	3,263
− 4,235	− 7,428	− 2,888	− 1,404

2,103	7,397	6,007	6,707
− 1,943	− 2,226	− 2,436	− 3,248

3,341	9,379	4,084	5,093
− 1,896	− 3,913	− 1,437	− 2,754

Name: _____

4-Digi Subtraction(7)

9,334	9,947	4,704	2,838
- 2,573	- 5,616	- 2,300	- 2,054

3,324	8,003	4,457	8,091
- 1,967	- 5,146	- 2,735	- 6,336

4,713	6,444	9,804	7,077
- 4,147	- 2,602	- 4,259	- 3,562

1,409	4,473	8,584	3,161
- 1,147	- 2,955	- 7,989	- 1,328

3,762	1,121	9,529	1,813
- 2,720	- 1,092	- 7,680	- 1,144

4-Digi Subtraction(8)

2,377	2,674	9,659	3,325
- 2,041	- 2,148	- 1,715	- 126

6,355	9,278	3,739	8,922
- 2,670	- 5,345	- 2,627	- 6,981

1,247	2,066	4,462	8,232
- 514	- 1,934	- 2,875	- 6,683

4,940	3,691	3,792	8,584
- 3,565	- 2,429	- 1,988	- 2,343

9,837	3,979	8,361	5,627
- 9,511	- 1,478	- 1,388	- 3,356

4-Digi Subtraction(9)

```
  7,611        435         423       6,765
- 1,816     -  327     -    106    - 3,866
```

```
    515        278       7,850      6,927
-   184     -  186     - 2,193    - 2,805
```

```
    963        179         457        470
-   450     -  101     -    360    -   148
```

```
  4,047      1,637       8,403        687
- 3,456     - 1,542    - 1,289    -   394
```

```
  4,161        348       8,317        148
- 3,587     -  277     - 3,194    -   115
```

4-Digi Subtraction(10)

6,267 - 6,168	854 - 629	7,872 - 7,505	2,474 - 1,633
310 - 160	774 - 680	7,527 - 4,551	602 - 310
156 - 136	9,457 - 2,813	3,150 - 2,323	8,074 - 529
9,297 - 1,116	898 - 252	589 - 317	6,794 - 3,701
3,348 - 2,235	2,527 - 1,098	847 - 192	365 - 216

4-Digi Subtraction(1)

```
  5,925          2,694          3,648          7,439
- 2,317        - 2,424        - 3,543        -   435
  3,608            270            105          7,004


  5,398          5,605          3,101          7,771
- 1,360        - 2,207        -   762        - 2,206
  4,038          3,398          2,339          5,565


  6,642          2,868          3,849          1,051
-   167        - 1,909        - 3,383        - 1,030
  6,475            959            466             21


  2,954          2,128          3,570          7,298
- 1,584        - 1,043        -   361        - 3,828
  1,370          1,085          3,209          3,470


  6,993          8,825          7,187          4,330
- 4,865        - 7,006        - 5,469        - 2,880
  2,128          1,819          1,718          1,450
```

Twenty-Five

4-Digi Subtraction(2)

3,250 - 209 **3,041**	9,843 - 1,626 **8,217**	4,134 - 2,479 **1,655**	4,508 - 1,580 **2,928**
1,286 - 1,199 **87**	2,767 - 1,480 **1,287**	7,841 - 2,299 **5,542**	9,519 - 5,273 **4,246**
6,227 - 3,591 **2,636**	1,784 - 611 **1,173**	5,245 - 2,576 **2,669**	7,948 - 3,414 **4,534**
3,560 - 531 **3,029**	4,818 - 2,215 **2,603**	2,464 - 1,984 **480**	9,870 - 1,178 **8,692**
9,005 - 1,356 **7,649**	9,380 - 8,459 **921**	7,748 - 7,120 **628**	8,401 - 2,280 **6,121**

Twenty-Six

4-Digi Subtraction(3)

9,717 - 7,350 **2,367**	8,622 - 1,897 **6,725**	9,163 - 2,838 **6,325**	3,228 - 1,751 **1,477**
3,306 - 3,286 **20**	2,594 - 1,038 **1,556**	6,671 - 4,567 **2,104**	5,714 - 5,123 **591**
4,978 - 2,407 **2,571**	4,062 - 852 **3,210**	4,676 - 2,573 **2,103**	8,170 - 4,483 **3,687**
1,200 - 1,028 **172**	5,881 - 5,548 **333**	3,672 - 2,612 **1,060**	4,342 - 3,640 **702**
7,617 - 6,038 **1,579**	7,942 - 6,530 **1,412**	1,982 - 622 **1,360**	4,006 - 1,177 **2,829**

27

Twenty-Seven

4-Digi Subtraction(4)

8,997	8,964	9,298	7,150
- 4,666	- 4,495	- 7,418	- 6,432
4,331	**4,469**	**1,880**	**718**

5,420	4,912	9,907	2,094
- 4,459	- 3,974	- 3,640	- 1,204
961	**938**	**6,267**	**890**

9,447	6,606	2,850	3,824
- 5,487	- 6,410	- 1,762	- 2,981
3,960	**196**	**1,088**	**843**

7,428	6,403	3,551	7,831
- 5,669	- 2,186	- 601	- 2,694
1,759	**4,217**	**2,950**	**5,137**

8,906	4,457	6,853	9,738
- 8,041	- 1,411	- 6,761	- 1,934
865	**3,046**	**92**	**7,804**

Twenty-Eight

4-Digi Subtraction(5)

2,654 - 2,116 **538**	547 - 494 **53**	618 - 541 **77**	320 - 188 **132**
3,797 - 2,390 **1,407**	500 - 278 **222**	727 - 698 **29**	301 - 136 **165**
8,529 - 3,316 **5,213**	2,153 - 2,083 **70**	375 - 139 **236**	182 - 34 **148**
9,329 - 398 **8,931**	662 - 40 **622**	6,103 - 4,154 **1,949**	1,001 - 184 **817**
2,062 - 1,432 **630**	1,323 - 1,122 **201**	7,218 - 4,832 **2,386**	450 - 23 **427**

29

Twenty-Nine

4-Digi Subtraction(6)

3,514 - 1,207 **2,307**	7,511 - 3,116 **4,395**	3,453 - 1,047 **2,406**	9,973 - 1,410 **8,563**
2,594 - 2,334 **260**	4,664 - 2,274 **2,390**	6,102 - 5,818 **284**	7,681 - 3,963 **3,718**
4,626 - 4,235 **391**	7,914 - 7,428 **486**	5,436 - 2,888 **2,548**	3,263 - 1,404 **1,859**
2,103 - 1,943 **160**	7,397 - 2,226 **5,171**	6,007 - 2,436 **3,571**	6,707 - 3,248 **3,459**
3,341 - 1,896 **1,445**	9,379 - 3,913 **5,466**	4,084 - 1,437 **2,647**	5,093 - 2,754 **2,339**

Thirty

4-Digi Subtraction(7)

```
   9,334        9,947        4,704        2,838
 - 2,573      - 5,616      - 2,300      - 2,054
   6,761        4,331        2,404          784


   3,324        8,003        4,457        8,091
 - 1,967      - 5,146      - 2,735      - 6,336
   1,357        2,857        1,722        1,755


   4,713        6,444        9,804        7,077
 - 4,147      - 2,602      - 4,259      - 3,562
     566        3,842        5,545        3,515


   1,409        4,473        8,584        3,161
 - 1,147      - 2,955      - 7,989      - 1,328
     262        1,518          595        1,833


   3,762        1,121        9,529        1,813
 - 2,720      - 1,092      - 7,680      - 1,144
   1,042           29        1,849          669
```

Thirty-One

4-Digi Subtraction(8)

```
  2,377        2,674        9,659        3,325
- 2,041      - 2,148      - 1,715      -   126
─────────    ─────────    ─────────    ─────────
    336          526        7,944        3,199


  6,355        9,278        3,739        8,922
- 2,670      - 5,345      - 2,627      - 6,981
─────────    ─────────    ─────────    ─────────
  3,685        3,933        1,112        1,941


  1,247        2,066        4,462        8,232
-   514      - 1,934      - 2,875      - 6,683
─────────    ─────────    ─────────    ─────────
    733          132        1,587        1,549


  4,940        3,691        3,792        8,584
- 3,565      - 2,429      - 1,988      - 2,343
─────────    ─────────    ─────────    ─────────
  1,375        1,262        1,804        6,241


  9,837        3,979        8,361        5,627
- 9,511      - 1,478      - 1,388      - 3,356
─────────    ─────────    ─────────    ─────────
    326        2,501        6,973        2,271
```

Thirty-Two

4-Digi Subtraction(9)

```
   7,611          435            423          6,765
 - 1,816        -  327         -  106        - 3,866
   5,795          108            317          2,899


     515          278          7,850          6,927
 -   184        -  186        - 2,193        - 2,805
     331           92          5,657          4,122


     963          179            457            470
 -   450        -  101        -  360         -  148
     513           78             97            322


   4,047        1,637          8,403            687
 - 3,456        - 1,542        - 1,289        -  394
     591           95          7,114            293


   4,161          348          8,317            148
 - 3,587        -  277         - 3,194        -  115
     574           71          5,123             33
```

Thirty-Three

4-Digi Subtraction(10)

```
  6,267          854         7,872         2,474
- 6,168        - 629       - 7,505       - 1,633
     99          225           367           841


    310          774         7,527           602
-   160        - 680       - 4,551       -   310
    150           94         2,976           292


    156        9,457         3,150         8,074
-   136      - 2,813       - 2,323       -   529
     20        6,644           827         7,545


  9,297          898           589         6,794
- 1,116        - 252       -   317       - 3,701
  8,181          646           272         3,093


  3,348        2,527           847           365
- 2,235      - 1,098       -   192       -   216
  1,113        1,429           655           149
```

Thirty-Four

70241999R00069

Made in the USA
San Bernardino, CA
26 February 2018